Honduras

by Shira Zwiren

Consultant: Karla Ruiz
Teacher's College, Columbia University
New York, New York

New York, New York

Credits

Cover, © Alejandro Rivera/iStock and Rafal Cichawa/Shutterstock; 3, © RestonImages/Shutterstock; 4, © Robert English/Shutterstock; 5T, © John Hamlon/Shutterstock; 5B, © HenryRomero/REUTERS/Newscom; 7, © dstephens/iStock; 8, © dstephens/iStock; 9T, © dstephens/iStock; 9B, © RoatanTrav/iStock; 10, © gary yim/Shutterstock; 10B, © Edwin Butter/Shutterstock; 11T, © Shawn Jackson/Dreamstime; 11B, © Pictureguy/Shutterstock; 12–13, © T photography/Shutterstock; 13B, © Rafal Cichawa/Shutterstock; 14, © Africa Studio/Shutterstock; 15, © Nicholas Gill/Alamy Stock Photo; 16, © slhy/Shutterstock; 17, © guvendemir/iStock; 18T, © Iurii Kachkovskyi/Shutterstock; 18B, © branislavpudar/Shutterstock; 19, © mojo_jojo/Fotolia; 20–21, © mtcurado/iStock; 22, © Blend Images/Shutterstock; 23, © Nicholas Gill/Alamy Stock Photo; 24, © Yulia Furman/Shutterstock; 25T, © Dolly MJ/Shutterstock; 25B, © siamionau pavel/Shutterstock; 26–27, © JORGE CABRERA/REUTERS/Newscom; 27B, © Martin Battiti/Dreamstime; 28–29, © mooinblack/Shutterstock; 29B, © irin-k/Shutterstock; 30T, © Oleg_Mit/Shutterstock and © Asaf Eliason/Shutterstock; 30B, © Brian Atkinson/Alamy Stock Photo; 31(T to B), © charliechanel/123RF, © Nicholas Gill/Alamy Stock Photo, © JORGE CABRERA/REUTERS/Newscom, © Ttstudio/Shutterstock, © AustralianCamera/Shutterstock, and © Sam Chadwick/Shutterstock; 32, © Daniel-Alvarez/Shutterstock.

Publisher: Kenn Goin
Editor: Jessica Rudolph
Creative Director: Spencer Brinker
Design: Debrah Kaiser
Photo Researcher: Olympia Shannon

Library of Congress Cataloging-in-Publication Data

Names: Zwiren, Shira, author.
Title: Honduras / by Shira Zwiren.
Description: New York, New York : Bearport Publishing, [2017] | Series:
  Countries we come from | Includes bibliographical references and index. |
  Audience: Ages 6–10.
Identifiers: LCCN 2016007662 (print) | LCCN 2016008036 (ebook) | ISBN
  9781944102708 (library binding) | ISBN 9781944102906 (ebook)
Subjects: LCSH: Honduras—Juvenile literature.
Classification: LCC F1503.2 .Z85 2017 (print) | LCC F1503.2 (ebook) | DDC
  972.83—dc23
LC record available at http://lccn.loc.gov/2016007662

For more information, write to Bearport Publishing Company, Inc., 45 West 21st Street, Suite 3B, New York, New York 10010. Printed in the United States of America.

10 9 8 7 6 5 4 3 2

Contents

This Is Honduras

Warm

BRIGHT

Exciting

Honduras is a country in Central America.

More than eight million people live there.

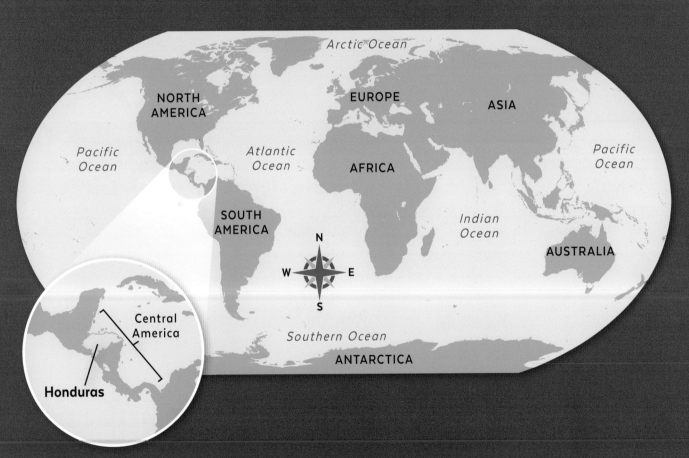

Honduras has many small islands.

Honduras is very beautiful.
Sandy beaches line the coasts.

Rivers flow through thick **rain forests**.

Tall mountains rise up in the middle of the country.

Most Hondurans live in towns in the mountains.

Honduras is home to interesting animals. Monkeys live in rain forests.

Sea turtles swim in the sea.

The white-tailed deer is the national animal of Honduras. It can leap 30 feet (9 m)!

Honduras has a long history.

About 2,000 years ago, the Maya people built a huge city called Copán (koh-PAHN).

Today, nobody lives in the city.

Scientists study **ruins** in Copán to learn about the Maya.

The Spanish came to Honduras in the 1500s.

They ruled for 300 years.

They dug **mines** to look for gold and silver.

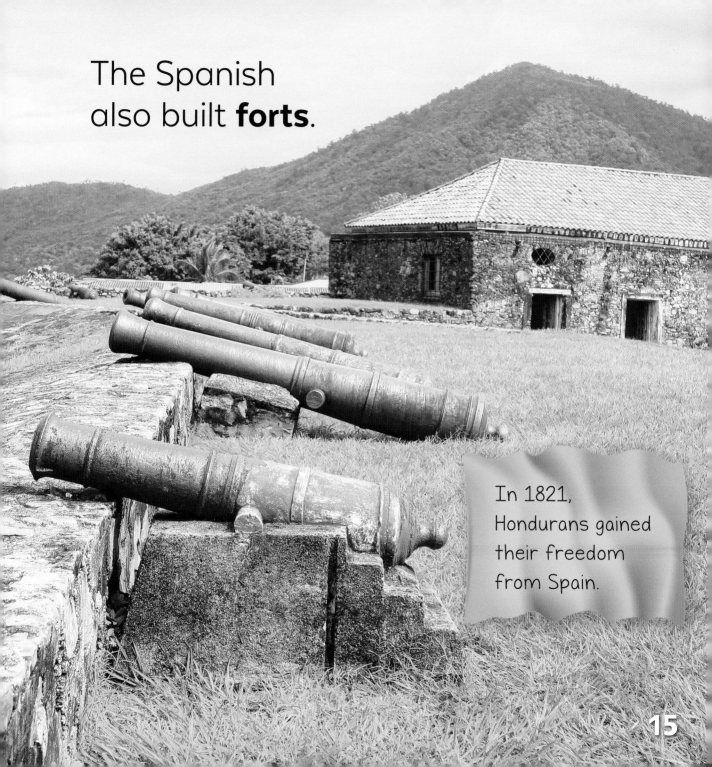

The Spanish also built **forts**.

In 1821, Hondurans gained their freedom from Spain.

Hondurans speak Spanish.

This is how you say *good morning* in Spanish:

Buenos días
(BWAY-nohs DEE-ahs)

This is how you say *good night*:

Buenas noches
(BWAY-nahs NOH-chayz)

Many people in Honduras also speak English.

Farmers in Honduras grow foods such as bananas and corn.

Many foods grown in Honduras are sold in the United States.

Farmers also raise cows and sheep.

The **capital** of Honduras is Tegucigalpa (tay-goo-see-GAHL-pah).

It's also the country's largest city.

Many young people go to college in the capital.

Most Hondurans are Catholic.

As part of their religion, parents choose *compadres* (cohm-PAH-drays) for their newborn baby.

Compadres are godparents.

Compadres give guidance to the child as he or she grows up.

a Catholic church
in Honduras

Hondurans eat tasty foods like tamales.

Tamales are made from ground-up corn called cornmeal.

cornmeal

The cornmeal is stuffed with meat, cheese, or fruit.

Then it's wrapped in a banana leaf and cooked.

wrapped tamales

Beans and rice is another popular meal.

Hondurans celebrate lots of holidays.

Independence day is September 15.

People celebrate their freedom with parades.

Christmas is also a big holiday. People set off fireworks on Christmas Eve.

Many Hondurans love to play soccer.

Almost every town in Honduras has its own soccer team!

In Honduras, soccer is called *fútbol* (FOOT–bohl).

Fast Facts

Capital city:
Tegucigalpa

Population of Honduras:
More than eight million

Main language:
Spanish

Money: Lempira

Major religion: Roman Catholic

Neighboring countries:
Guatemala, El Salvador, and Nicaragua

Cool Fact: The money in Honduras is called Lempira. It is named after a native chief who fought against Spanish rule in the 1500s.

Glossary

capital (KAP-uh-tuhl) a city where a country's government is based

forts (FORTS) strong buildings made to protect an area from attacks

independence (in-di-PEN-duhnss) freedom

mines (MINEZ) underground tunnels built to search for minerals, such as gold

rain forests (RAYN FOR-ists) warm, wet places where many trees grow

ruins (ROO-inz) the remains of something that has collapsed or been destroyed

31

Index

Read More

Frazel, Ellen. *Honduras (Exploring Countries).* Minneapolis, MN: Bellwether Media (2013).

Kras, Sara Louise. *Honduras (Enchantment of the World).* New York: Scholastic (2006).

Learn More Online

To learn more about Honduras, visit
www.bearportpublishing.com/CountriesWeComeFrom

About the Author

Shira Zwiren is a writer who loves learning about the world. She lives in New York with her husband and hilarious two-year-old daughter.